Such Rich Hour

KUHL HOUSE POETS    *edited by Jorie Graham and Mark Levine*

# Such Rich Hour

POEMS BY COLE SWENSEN

*University of Iowa Press* ᴪ IOWA CITY

University of Iowa Press, Iowa City 52242
Copyright © 2001 by Cole Swensen
All rights reserved
Printed in the United States of America

Design by Richard Eckersley

http://www.uiowa.edu/~uipress

The publication of this book was
generously supported by the University
of Iowa Foundation.

Printed on acid-free paper

Library of Congress Cataloging-in-Publication Data
Swensen, Cole, 1955–
Such rich hour: poems / by Cole Swensen
p.   cm.—(Kuhl House poets)
ISBN 0-87745-775-1 (pbk.)
1. Très riches heures du duc de Berry—Poetry.
2. Manuscripts, Latin (Medieval and modern)—Poetry.
3. Catholic Church—Liturgy—Poetry.
4. Fifteenth century—Poetry. 5. Berry (France)—Poetry.
6. Book of hours—Poetry. 7. Church year—Poetry.
8. Months—Poetry. I. Title. II. Series.
PS3569.W384 S8    2001
811'.54dc21                            2001027471

01  02  03  04  05  P  5  4  3  2  1

*To Hilton, with love,*
*this story of a hundred years.*

# Contents

# Acknowledgments

*American Letters & Commentary:*
   "October 4, 1451: Nicholas of Cusa Preaches at Aix-la-Chapelle,"
   "October 15, 1415: Guild Initiation: Paolo Uccello Examines the Sky"

*Boston Book Review:*
   "October: A Superstitious Hour,"
   "January 29, 1408: The Great Flood Of,"
   "August 17, 1427: The first record of Gypsies in Europe"

*Boston Review:*
   "Preface,"
   "Recipes for Red"

*Chicago Review:*
   "When Bells Were Named,"
   "The Invention of Equal Hours,"
   "November 1: All Saints' Day"

*Conjunctions:*
   "March 1: Spring Agriculture,"
   "March 3,"
   "May 1, 1 A.M.: Les Revenants,"
   "May 1: Broad Day,"
   "May 30, 1427: Joan-not-yet-saint with Sheep,"
   "June 1: Reaping,"
   "October 1, 1445,"
   "October 2"

*Cutbank:*
   "January 17: St. Antony's Day: Les Flammes,"
   "June 24: A Long Day"

*Facture:*

"January 3: The Feast of St. Genevieve,"
"February 14, 1404: The Birth of Leon Battista Alberti,"
"The Fourth Month: April: with Preview of Joan of Arc,"
"May 19, 1435: The Great Freeze"

*Fence:*

"January 28: St. Thomas,"
"March 25, 1472/75: *The Annunciation*, Leonardo da Vinci,"
"Early Morning: Ours of the Wholly Spirit"

*Five Fingers Review:*

"April 25: Day of St. Mark, patron of vellum"

*The Germ:*

"September 1.618: In Light of Gold,"
"October 28, 1449: The Translation of the Relics of St. Jean,"
"Fortune, *Boccaccio* of John the Fearless"

*New American Writing:*

"The Painter Paints a Calendar,"
"February 19, 1414: First Appearance of the Whooping Cough,"
"August 1427: Abundance,"
"The Evolution of the Garden"

*Rhizome:*

"February 2: The Benediction of the Candles,"
"March: Nocturne,"
"April 2: Feast Day of Francis of Paola, Patron Saint of Seafarers,"
"The Machine Designs" as "The Increasing Intricacy of the Machine"

Such Rich Hour

# Prologue

*And ten days later, the locks and keys*
*to the city of Paris were changed* (1405) you will die
eleven years later of plague)
       were made
       Captains of the city of Paris
       Mes Sieurs de Berry et de Bourbon
entièrement dit      You
(toi aussi
that death is an angle with grey eyes
I read it somewhere;
therefore,
come true.
(if you only)    le least idée      of that qui doit arriver
(mon âme)
it is said
"it is sown" though there is no
reason, particularly,
that it had to happen/will happen (circle one) this way.

# Preface

numbers, which Saint Augustine considered
                          God thinks
if he am is therefore there

I remember liking the sun

he said. He was
interviewed in Green Park on Sunday he said, I remember very clearly
to be the thoughts of God. Saint Augustine and thank
there's one
who
exempt
held and can
you imagine
what

he too had a face no he

1 through 12

basic, they seemed
cardinal, seminal, eyes nose mouth and
there are seven ways into      unless you      count the fact that

she said it's only a

it was only a

very tiny slice. Saint

Augustine breathed

at the top of his lungs he still thinks
of numbers as the thoughts of God

counting

is the body of thinking if thinking when thickened takes on

certain fingerprints on the edge of the door, on the doorjamb: determined:
premerchand: premedititian: internal
examination = does not equal
they had a word for:

Extermination. Said we yes, no,
                              oh, some other
seems we were after
groceries.
1,
2,
3,    7, 9, let me/eat those grains of sand//I the one who flid/who flied/who
can
          if burned palms as now crowned if done

with

said

I'm going to count to ten                    (fiery breath) we will

consider the proposition/inquire of the cross-section, the minute dedication
to empty the ocean to fill in the sand.

# Introduction

The following poems are based on the *Très Riches Heures du Duc de Berry,* a fifteenth-century book of hours. Books of hours were popular during the Middle Ages as personal devotional texts designed to allow individuals to observe religious ritual outside the strict format of the mass. The *Très Riches Heures* is one of the most elaborate of the genre and, furthermore, epitomizes the International Gothic style, a composite of influences from all over Europe. It flourished particularly in Paris, which, because of its strong patronage of the arts, attracted artists in great numbers toward the end of the fourteenth and beginning of the fifteenth centuries.

This confluence of artistic trends accompanied an influx of cultural, philosophical, and social ideas, which in turn coincided with a period of political and natural turmoil. In brief, the fifteenth century in France swung from recurrent plague, the Hundred Years' War, and a civil war to the development of perspective, the perfection of the clock, and the emergence of printing. Its rate, magnitude, and variety of change look extreme even from a post–twentieth century point of view.

A word more on this particular manuscript—it was commissioned by Jean, Duc de Berry, the son of one king (Jean le Bon), brother of another (Charles V), and uncle of a third (Charles VI). He had wealth and power, and to him, fine books were the proper expression of both. During his life, he commissioned six books of hours, of which the *Très Riches Heures* is the last and the most elaborate. For its execution, he gathered three of the best contemporary painters—Jean, Pol, and Herman Limbourg, brothers from Flanders. Unfortunately, all three brothers and the duc himself died in 1416, probably of the plague, leaving the book unfinished. It was completed in 1485 by Jean Colombe, one of the most accomplished illuminators of his day, though there is evidence that another, unidentified painter also did extensive work on it around midcentury.

The poems that follow begin as a response to this manuscript, and specifically to the calendar section that opens this and all traditional books of hours. The calendar lists the principal saints' days and other important religious holidays of the medieval year in a given region. In keeping with the cyclical rhythm of a calendar, the poems follow the sequence of days and months and not necessarily that of years.

Poems titled the first of a given month bear a relation to the *Très Riches Heures* calendar illustration for that month, though they are not dependent upon it. Rather, they—like all the pieces here—soon diverge from their source and simply wander the century. And finally, they are simply collections of words, each of which begins and ends on the page itself.

Similarly, references to the Hundred Years' War and other specific events do not require a run to an encyclopedia, but will instead, I hope, contribute to the life-in-lore of these events, a life that gives another, parallel life to all that occurs. However, those interested in pursuing the history of the period and/or the images themselves will find a list of sources at the end.

After it was completed, the *Très Riches Heures* "disappeared" until 1855, when it was discovered in a girls' boarding school in Genoa. Just where it went during the intervening centuries has not been precisely determined, though what information there is suggests that it had an active life, with guest appearances in nobles' houses throughout Europe. It is now in the Musée Condé in Chantilly, where it is not available for public view; it has become so valuable that it has had to be locked away.

# Foreword

That mine that was a country, a
poverty starred
                      possession all
something
                              had a hoe deep in
deepening
                    breaking off the anchor
                    in the throe

"to him who sows"

but that's our secret. folded, hidden
the what you had—this made us

(aim and own) hover and row
we are
honing in on season:
                              may be and barely seem

(what I had heard
that you had won
                    my always did
thus onward        could

have died

or called

or stood

any (act)

but that you did

not look back.

# Forward

nunc
we videmus
see
darkly darkly we        through a glass        (there was this once)
           dark was        we see
dark as        thus is, and glass    glass  (sharp)
                             (dark) (are)

aenigmate aenigmate (we)(are) (is *was*)
(as in: *we saw*)      and this was also glass  *but face to face*
but ad faciem        be
per speculum    Corinthia
            incunabula
            (adoration of)
                (inveterae)    fa      ci      e
facie
facie
Gloria   (gloria)
tunc
tunc
autem
ad faciem
*si*

# January 1: The Feast of the New Year

Vows, a fête of, phalanx of, flagrant and sky all written on in snow: *hommage*
The duke sits,

waits

what

did you expect

= feast

did not mistake

just what

= eternity.       (the soft brush) how long it can/can it

*aproche + aproche*     (scatter the century)

last.

# January 1: Once Framed

the walls break down       never were      sugar in a storm    castle on a
verge.  are you ours?   are you all?

              *"aproche + aproche"*


           We one
king and  wielded, welded all our swan (plural) (upper right) (against red
was was once a sky)           (The sky was once a red thing,
             once unreeled)


(they say the face


        too is a wheel) (Read: We


        Turn back. Smile.      My
        Anonymous    cum-Angelus:   My Saint Why-
can-you-see-through-heaven


        of stars all afternoon
        do Shine. (Or 'shy'—I can't quite read the note, the
      faded ink, the quick break
in the smile.
"You could say we say we invented the sky as a blue *could* that we loved till
we choked. So what

are you doing sobbing through the feast, what with all the women dancing,
the colors running, the men carving meat.

9

## January 3: The Feast of St. Genevieve; patron saint of Paris; 422–500

blew the candle out no devil knew not
the name stopped

them at the gates       of the city stood
Huns by the thousands and the candle

            Conflagrate:


            And thousands
dust.        The hosts
sat down to dinner by candlelight     her barley bread
and beans and all the horror of
(in flames)       (will come again)
         riding out in battle to be embraced,
     a surfeit of
white and shone
stone by stone across these fields
        blows      out the candle
     against the window, which
catches fire:
     Her tongue alone can cure the plague. Her hair
a single strand
replace a river in a pinch of salt. A barge coming upstream
laden down. Give me your city in a million little bones. Mine
she says were removed without the slightest negative effect & the skin re-
sewn with the blindman's stitch.

# The Painter Paints a Calendar

Languor. Succor. Ardor. Such is the tenor of the entry. You open a little door.
The door could be anywhere.


And laid there a face. For instance, at certain points, no longer wishing or able
        to emulate Rome,
they began the year at Christmas for example or
                        the Annunciation or Easter in all its moving
target and borrows
        from the inclination of passing
                suns, seasons, moons that may or may
not occur again
        (we repeat)
        (because it seems)
     Begin:
     Here he put their faces
            which were all
his.


     (I rise eye by eye; I fissure plains.)

And repeat (again) (because it seems)
Begin: and whose will linger
whose wither
what king might    made of    mine he said. A window

is just a window    looking out on a vast
delicate brush    catches the ear of the sun
across the year, which, too, keeps slipping: errant prince, anchor
in the wish, a wristful of deed:    I've    (paint therefore I
see)
always
wanted

he said
and did.

# When Bells Were Named

And wake up to

The Hour of the Bells           Each one and then rang

"To name an object is
        "to event"
     and to yet
           that reaches out
             that must
distill to ghost
        its want of all the almost lived.

We'd wake up early and watch the sky rend.

          They say (cf. Huizinga Ch. 1) that
people felt more deeply then, that
people raged; they careened, shredding the sky into streamers the color of

One bell for every hour. One name for every bell. One

day it rained and sounded like a mouth
had welded a tongue. What is soft
       is what remains
       strung up. What hung there when you stopped,
drop-jawed. They say
(then France had
1,700,000 bells) you spoke
every language in the known world
which

back over its shoulder looked and did
you recognize the source. Did
you catch your breath and what

                                        wait? what

worth?  (once)

the sky, gold, then red, then gold again and again
                                        the vein
                                                in the laboring hand
raised the hand (is, they say,
                music at its most refined) the raised hand waved, it
                                        rang.

## January 5 ÷ 5

= One. Need say we     what was that     you said     it shrank
to a point

and the point reigned     ever divisible
unto     beyond, and beyond the

hour of the intimate, conjugate, annihilate, throned

any number of other     wherefore innumerable.     Who
     said/equated/constructed
The circle as the sweep that turns back before the arc: Look
at what I found ("One day I saw you one (and how we could go on) (Father,
Ghost, and half a million men) fused (like opposites do: When & when. And
& and     Snow.     Fear.
Year.
Fury.
Snow.

15

# January 6, 1400: The Founding of *La Cour Amoureuse*
—a literary and legal association dedicated to poetic
creation and the honor of women

Cold,
       bored,
              and underfoot, thin
                    ice (glance
                         down and the face is reflected is
unowned, today is
             all we can see
             is
             frost in the trees, étinceling, pricks the
         skin but still can't remember the

old order crumbling
the feudal piety of orchestrated certainties: "To pass
the time more graciously in the raging midst of plague." Erect
                               upon humility
and loyalty
specific offices including:
             the four *"Concierges of the Gardens and Orchards of*
*Love"*
and 32 recording secretaries
"The early literary societies were modeled on the older orders of chivalry
keenly acutely
recognized love as representation within the highly organized life of the court
of something missing
                     Jean de Berry: "One must say
                     the one and do the
other of unconscionable red, who unasked, who, undeterred, said
yes.

# Response: Christine

de Pisan founds (inciting

the "first literary quarrel in French history") The
Order of the Rose; 1402:

Jean
de Meun
has in
his
has
Jean de Montreuil (be damned) Jean
le Sénéchal, for example, asks

*Le*

no on his lips


*débat de deux amants*                    i.e., once upon

the mind a spring and a tongue
                    (said what woman *would*, or ever,
in the long run, did. (And by 'done' we mean
who (what) came (is just now coming) in.

# January 6: St. Matthew's Day

as the Magi stood before Herod and said
                                 further home,
             ask
directions of none.        "Turn left."
and replied having hammered our fingers from gold, having honed and
had themselves also heard:
*ecce Magi ab Oriente venerunt*
though not so sudden was

arrival is
after all a slow

and on the ground, this (all over the ground)
that

stars fall sometimes and
there you are
up to your knees in light
*ab Oriente verdant mendicant*

and once I thought
my horse would bolt, but,
though blinded, he did not, but
                        (and not a mark on him) stood
                        calmly eating the burning grass.

# January 17: St. Antony's Day: Les Flammes

"There's a disease that eats up the limbs that feels like ants are eating them" *(St. Antoine! St. Antoine . . .)* and
there was a disease that dried up the heart from the inside out, and another that
began as spots of light on the skin that grew and grew and then enormously died.
Did you notice—all the saints died—sometimes in droves, and there was a disease
that made the body soar and one that made it disappear slowly,
grain by grain while
you watched.     (Fascinated. As in nailed to the spot.)
                                        (When you can see right through
the skull, there's still time, but you can't     (as in entranced
            affixed)
There's a grave just large enough for the face.


And a tendency incessantly to walk back and forth
and another to arrive. In the peripheral field, an impression of light that,
like all things, can't be named
                              (all living takes place
            (just before the word
            was said
            was hidden (or slid, envelope-style)
into fire or flood, but usually fire.

# January 28: St. Thomas

This day a great theophany
internaling an only<br>shining face

"Face the entire body
in light"

which is the book of his book<br>this make of his all

and Thomas Aquinas replied,
"The earth is made of dirt."

and he replied,
"things which give pleasure when they are perceived are called
beautiful. And herein lies the problem.
Skin covers wrist, sea, dearth. I was caught counting and thus put to death.

Meaning water, or lover of water, or both.

# January 29, 1408: The Great Flood Of

To a life of moving water
and a watermark on the water
                    someone (a woman) watching
                                        (and move
            me have I
            told you how you
        much "River,
river, on the

Refuse to answer
                "I
looked out my window
            and saw falling through the rain in sheets
                                    standing on the bank
as the water rose and bridge after bridge (all three:
*Le Petit, Le Grand,* and *Le Neuf* (now le Pont St. Michel) fell and what sound
will atone. Atonish.
            Embellish/Embitter/Embark: To a moving life. She watched
a cup and saucer spin for a moment on the surface.

# February 1: Winter Agriculture

And here to our left we see . . .

the hand "of the unknown as it paints the unknown."
*A name held locked     below the tongue*
*does not unknot        inside the grave.*

*And said stave off      (this polished and)*
*with an endless bought   from the silence of snow*

*and then given back.*

The basic techniques
of apiculture haven't changed since etc. and then we go into
the anatomy of the bee—how its legs frangere in their private foray, splinter like
the feathered bones inside the finger drifting. And how, and then how, the laces
drawn through error and we hear, throughout the threaded hallways, their move-
ments leadened into season and that bees were first domesticated by nomadic
tribes on the Asian Steppes who used them initially as compasses, and then as
maps, my lady, we live in a tiny, tiny world.

# February 1 bis

"and the body between word and world fuses, frays"
(overheard)
no castle holds
it's a world whose white

                                    wouldn't you have thought
white trees white sun white blood that plummets from the skin, hunches in
the heart
            has not been spared


The ink has bled
            through from the back of the page to
                        landscape,
                        in this case,
                              a man

                hauling wood
                asks directions


She says


Hand me your needle please mine pricks and makes
my hearing acute:
                  if
                  Somewhere
in the picture it's winter, bird-
like and the birds are voracious
                        A man

is hauling wood up the slope,
the click of the gate in the yard,
the footsteps leading up to it
all by themselves, hives.

# February 2: The Benediction of the Candles

when the faithful go marked
forehead in ashes washes
the bones beneath the very
and ground atone for scrubbing           and in the future my body
this body already

                dust to dust           must to must
                break to stun           that one already has

borne all foreseen
takes place one Tuesday morning when we at the local fountain washing and
out of which came the molten stone that will be from now on
something won

                (as in torn           out of)           and what
a strange shape for paradise. I thought it would be more round.

# The Invention of Equal Hours

Rare they
and approximate who
could tell the hour after
star after star in a heaven of moving parts
that do not break down to nonmoving parts                (a night
                                                                            x candles long

                    and tide go down
                    and raptor home
                    and wager then          each candle three to four hours
marked
and sputters out
as dawn threads a crack          through the glaze and breaks
the tiny jewels
against the tiny gears
of the barely here


of the stars turn whole and a whole black


sky of a clock


thread and sand and count


                                                    the leavened hours: now samed—
they say something's gained in the equal
            beyond
            a simple immunity to weather

*"And not until the end of the Middle Ages and the advent of societies of commercial
basis came the genesis of the equal hour and its mechanical registration"*

                    Before then bells had names.
You'd wake up in the middle of the night and find you'd been counting in
your sleep.

# February 4

and this in the middle
of the Hundred Years' War.

# February 14, 1404: The Birth of Leon Battista Alberti

As the first surviving account of a method of perspective construction, Alberti's brief description of how to draw a picture of a chequerboard floor has often been subjected to the kind of detailed, awe-stricken analysis usually reserved for Holy Writ. —J. V. Field


One-eyed ceiling
always vault                                saw converging
                        O = *oeil* =

a bottomless heaven peopled
                        strangers
                        brush
                                each other in passing, let
touch linger
without looking
at each                                if you arch
your hand
and hold it like this, hollowed
over the head of a stranger
from behind so that he does not see you                there is someone

at the window, a *"sheaf*
*of rays splays from eye to seen*

                                *that thus released*
                                *that keens the ken*
                                *that the picture therefore represents"*

according to which
with the abandon of                orthogonal bones (of the ceiling of the
                                hand) The face behind
            the fan becomes a fan.

## February 19, 1414: First Appearance of the Whooping Cough in Europe

All these cranes they say Omen as they might/as if A
triangular sky (Pray
        (won't you let me help you with that

white slice in (cf. white) (cf. within)

# March 1: Spring Agriculture

Thus we find triads: dimension, form, and order
substance, nature, power

and took (there were three brothers

every care and every caution:

green infused with grey
         indicates
         a cult of weather: you were born here were you born
vassal, slave, your only master
with the fingers of a weaver tied back the finite branches
with the fingers of a lover let the seed sift through his fingers

who so thereafter lived here. A small dog is running up to the road
in front of a flock of sheep in front of a large man carrying
something (we can't see what) (sheaf?) (shearing?) holding (soft)
against himself.

# Saturday, March 2

Mélusine, who was touched
beyond oath

and all ten sons

(dead) and the husband who

in jealousy
and fled
in
the form of

a dragon she turned
the sky red for a thousand years

"and the husband

who" blue
field, ten what

red? what

are you doing in my sky?

# March 3

father son and holy father son and only counting        if it gathers
can amount to or can turn
as has here        almost human.        You who would have thought or so
        you said        Who knew him later, carved
                a three-legged stool to go milking, a three-pronged fork
to go haying and the child born with three fingers on every hand and three hands
was allowed to live because and it all adds up: father, form & after; face, hand &
anger. Spherical. Uncial. Envelope you
                                                in
                                        and is
                its own and only weather
                        sounds like laughter.

# The Recurrent Miracle

*une si belle chance* that a
*merveille* could strike—
       death from a casual glance
       or triplets in the rue Anglais
            and asked permission of the Church
            to cut open the chest of the man who'd burst into flames
as he turned to reply
           "In the air"          all
that         where         we were
      the ones     the ragged wings     fell upon
                        and drowned
                        in
the middle of a spring afternoon. The neighbors watched
and wondered if anything would change.

## March 8 (Feast Day of John of God, Patron Saint of Printers), 1476: The first Bible printed in Paris

Moves the word is good of God what moving

small would       (just as we knew)        it did
wherever
          in my life is a moving life
whereupon
word and act, this one
          times one
          equals
               so what
               ever                you can shift
               at will             will
(they slip)
                    fix
                         at look        at anyone        still
          (be my heart        of
               (as God is to every
clockwork aviary.

# 1470: The first book printed in Paris

was not a Bible, but a book of private letters.

# March: Nocturne

and as are the nocturnes, three
in number bordered before and after by antiphon and
three lessons in            and as            darkness recited
to an end of night the many knees
kneeling and would forget
oneself and the rising voice
might have been many or any
other word for three:

> *thy name            in the whole            mindful            hast*
>
> *how forth firmament            of hands*
>
> *Lift up your gates O*
> *gates            shall enter in*

shall and.

# March 1432

so bitterly froze and the floodwaters reached
from the Place Maubert to the Place de Grève      undid
         half the Marché au Pain. We were stunned. We knew this meant.
and was an empty hand
           Item: there: some wrong is done      and avenged
       further on
from the Porte Saint-Antoine to the Porte Saint-Martin
                           from Noël to Pâques
                was nothing
in the markets that was green

two feet of ice on a river of sleeves

flood after freeze and flood again they are talking peace between kings.

# March 25: The Annunciation

Mary of the turning
              who turns around and stammers
      of the angry
      of the harried    Mary of the hurry        world of slightly falling
                                         shall know her
by her:
      hounded fountain
      folded garden
      inner lemon
      crown of stars
in a tower of stars                how often she looks up startled
                          at the thought      and says
              What are you doing in my house
What am I doing in my house?
              What am I doing?      and what am I incapable of doing?

# March 25, 1472/75:
## *The Annunciation,* Leonardo da Vinci

as in mid as in air as if there could
be enough
air
turns blue
All you have to do is walk away.

The railroad was invented
some 350 years later to explain
why things disappear

              so precisely
              pointed exactly

              blurs he said, we'll call

*fading perspective*
when the river erases

        to mountains the very     aerated
        birds turn ink

        grey
        with a blue tinge is called *color perspective* and has
something they say

        to do with oceans and refraction and all that goes
pale.

     It doesn't matter what they say. What who says what to whom.
Women in the choir fainting in the heat, falling back row by row. Or as they say
'falling out' a kind of fainting from belief off the edge of
        the
        combined
        become
*aerial perspective* as the initial inclination toward a compensation for the
capitulation to etherless space to
        empty space
        to
        emptiness

# The Evolution of the Garden

As Albertus Magnus instructs us

that shade is dearer than fruit      and the trees be not bitter ones      let them
not be
bitter please
pass me the sun

There were three distinct types of medieval garden: Ornamental, Orchard, and
Ones populated by animals and birds where we're allowed only in shadow and
falter

walking on windows: *hortus* in which *viridarium; virgultum*: Espalier the king
          with its
branches so arranged
that the fruit, ripening, mimes
the constellations and passes
                              through the entire zodiac in all the proper steps
                              : must be grafted:
                              apple, pear, manor, and
                              there go the deer! There were
carefully selected and ornamented spots for viewing
                                        all of geometry
                                        devolved from planting—
          the three:four:five triangular section
                              sang at night: *O*
*Master of the Embroidered Foliage* painting his eyeball green we were walking
through the fine tissue of which the ripping sound at the back of the picture on the
bottom of the world that
we could live here
                    *gardinum*
                    hundreds
                    of acres set aside for watching animals.

## March: The Third Lesson:
## to be said at night or upon rising

Cedar of Libanus, the exalted
                (as was I, oh L., a witness) a cypress
and a palm in Cades
                       In Jericho it was roses; on the plains an olive (I was
        and (believe me) just might
        if I say thee             is truly said to be happy. My palm, how
                unwoven, Mount Sion
and a single woman. (See Appendix.) There were no wounded
                          is risen the sun of justice
           and the cypress and the olive and the scar above the eye.

# April: In the Garden

The earth tilts, cracking open fields and the courtyard,
                    open,
          shows
what made by man, geometry in

form, and in division the plan,
nascent, of astronomy

                    But as for the men themselves, for instance,
the outlines of their hands recall only those of trees, everything
we love turns green. *Alain Roger:*
"Beauty in nature does not exist;
          it is we who weave it thus and thus believe it is
          just this: balance and thrust, a diamond placed
          in opposition to a triangle, divided
                              precisely,
                              precariously
                    the planets
will be so understood to interact:
          Luxembourg: Tuileries: Filigree: mathematical
not to please but to ease the mind: Square against three squares, sphere
                              within other spheres,
and the hand but paired.
Beauty is no less unlikely for having been invented.

# April 1, 1411: The Betrothal

This is how they lived: the dialogue was staged
and every woman given thus            thus said
Pardon me.                    Most probably: Lady A: Bonne d'Armagnac (grand-
                              daughter of Sir Duke) (looks at the ring which came
                              from another world and makes circles with her fingers
                              in the air. And He: (again, only a guess): duc Charles
                              d'Orléans, who being a poet said "Danger, je la voie
                              briefment, / Et que de sa bouche me die: / 'Ami, pensez
                              que seulement / C'estes vous de qui suis amie'" and
                              meant

in a field of green (read: early love)(ground from the malachite of
Hungary) wearing blue (both) (doth bet Fidelity against Eternity) made of
lapis lazuli brought
        all the way back from the Black Sea, which (they say) really is black.

# April 2: Feast Day of Francis of Paola, Patron Saint of Seafarers: The Astrolabe & Navigation

I do here suspend the here and this:
Wood
from this its sister circle: Circle.    Drop

and every star thus struck or did yes we did          believe that we
had marked
every star its course     and could we not          be so different nor
Go to sea
I said and drew faces on the back:          Sun, Moon, Mars, Note how
                                             it, relentless, tracks, plans
and by the rete will find

each day built of but
a series of hours
                        even the ocean
                                        sown divisible          and hold
the astrolabe in the hand, free of all inventor
and possibly too of invention, my son
drowned.

*History:*          Sorcery: (Once there were) a third century, a B.C.E., and
                    Greece. Held it up unto the face, held the
face up
unto that and this, the "what became." See therein the architectural trace,
the keen
eye at the very least the precise
                                        was
                                        no waste of sky
stowed
and ransomed back:     this built of my hand
            a palm
of prehensile lines, filigrate lines

I knew a man who made signs in the air and they stayed.
There are three things that are no good at sea.

*Technology:*      Take a wooden disk, suspend from a ring (iron, sudden, or
                        something  driven). Drop and watch. Who did not
The quite of late, with the stars countable on the face of things. You get
used to these things.

# April 3

Curve
now my
love these trees, three
careful arcs
arching away

from
create the space of

the way that turning your back on

The small
trees that border worlds on

Two men alone in boats.

# April 4, 1400

4 = 3 + 1 = trinity (holy) fused to (ideal) unity (or multiplicity ruptured by essentialism) or 2 squared—mirror & mirroring mirrored (note the parents in the picture looking on as they are mimicked: geometric as opposed to arithmetic progression. The four corners of the world, its elements times its humors times the ages of man: the four rivers of Paradise from which flowed Paradise into the four seasons that still reign at the four cardinal points where the four evangelists stand in place of the four letters in the name Adam and the four letters in the word 'name' and those in the word 'word' and in the word four and in hour, in ours, in honor, horror and scream. It's Spring. March divided by May.

And this at the height
of the plague.

## April 25: Day of St. Mark, patron of vellum: manufacture and preparation

veinèd day; the daylight through
                              *water, water*
(and opens the skin)
                    scraped in the sun

      that the words bleed toward
                                   paper animals of folded milk
      entire translucent herds)
                                   to their own reverse
                   *mirror mirror*
      centuries later

soaked in lye for fourteen days      then fourteen again
with the water running
                              over the hand
                              the words spill into
                   the framed sun
            of the page
         remembers
in its
            I can see
            through my little skin window
of the mouth of God
                   of the unborn calf
                   turning gold.

## The Fourth Month: April:
## with Preview of Joan of Arc

To: Land, air, and water. Must be added fire. Is utterly altered by fire. Are
altered entire. And is element only and in fact the
only element, only earthly example of four-dimensional form
                    hour by hour; I suppose it's true and must
          aligned with
          that ensure, that erased                    inherent in (the very notion of)
                                            time. I'd rather live in the cold.
The sky was red, the hours invented and then bent to serve. Someone.
          Hears.


                              An arbitrary machine called Heaven, a
silent engine, a single woman

said no, it heals, said the flames seal something I was just about to think
                    anneals. I see an edge.

# May 1, 1 A.M.: Les Revenants

*Old and on / certain nights of the Walpurgis*                    I saw them
                                                                  coming
                                                                  back
                                          that live

                            on bridges

            suspended


*". . . for centuries, ghosts were the exclusive privilege of the very wealthy and of*
*saints."*
Forgive
my apprehension
It stood
on a bridge slightly
swaying, vagary of wind,
tracery of sound that could have been wind
                                          carved. And refused
to leave. "Here lives
            what I did and cannot stop doing


*"Then suddenly by the 11th or 12th century, ghosts were all over, sometimes alone,*
*sometimes in great numbers, at first largely in dreams, but soon not so confined."*
                        (came back to *us*)
                                    (and thought I saw)
                        (as he was
                                    then
                                                the army of the dead called
*Maisnie Hellequin*—soldiers, children, women, saints, by the thousands
with all their attributes on


The moral was blatant ("There they go, paying") but we
were too distracted by their faces, how they hadn't changed at all and were
(in fact)                       more similar and were
                                        (the precision) there
                        by choice.


49

# May 1: Broad Day

note the curves         we pause and forth
                 and he turns
                 and she looks
down.
Start again:
       the forest whole in its gentle bow
           mirrored in color
           love was something we invented

         and perfectly enacted
"And made this body perfect
to the glory of the season: one bows low,
wears green,
gets made the center of a painting       made of crushed stone
                             (just grind and mix with
water) (called

         *verde azzurro*
to note its close connection with the azurite so common, also called
                     *chrysocolla*
                     *azurinum conversum*
*in viridem colorem*
                and
                *viride terrestre*
                though that is also
something else
something called "green earth"
               my love         who has promised the
but they weren't acute enough to make a landscape live
                 world
but did wonderfully as the base for the warm tones of the skin
                 when what I want
and were mixed with white alone in most works, though that too changed
       He turned
         toward a castle just visible beyond the trees,
and pointed and smiled, but I couldn't hear what he said.

# Early Morning: Ours of the Wholly Spirit

In sequential moment
follow glory and the glory to be
                nearly pointed out:
                            intervening mouth
Matins thus begins:
"Shalt open my lips without end
(kindle in them):
                  descent
                  brood
                  womb
                  wrought
                  quote
                  unquote face of the earth
(that it should have such and does and bend
over this child
              reigns
              without amen who lives.

# May 5: Earth, Air, Fire, Water, and Ether

As is the number
of man: four limbs and a heart, star-shaped if the star
                                         slanted were dwarfed
                                            to visibility, if to be
made in the image of the hand
                              and the hand itself
                              made to be splayed
                              to be made
                              suddenly life-sized
                    for whole moments at a time
there were five wounds to Christ of which

the fifth, shaped into the gaped gate of the womb, magnetic ellipse

          into another breast and thus
this extra

eclipse

in the year 840, May fifth, the 5
causing
the wheel to list thus
to never quite
rest as if
               my sun       my single one     and fell to pieces
is
a hand (what was held   (hold this   (my most urgent most     and
agile wound.

## May 9: Translation Day of Saint Nicholas of Myra, Patron Saint of Merchants, a Tuesday . . .

Called City of One Hundred Bell-Towers (not One Hundred Bells)
            By 1529, there were fifteen glovers
in the Place Saint-Séverin alone
the mills up and down the Seine and give
the air the air of a wheel in which

                                        the

                                        constantly turn, I am

                                                    this hilt,

that boat
coming up the river full of stone

                                        and herring from Le Havre

                        ground

                        in the circle grind            while

on the hill, the great mill vanes that keep the sky turning
its star-stropped dark into

                        here are         are hereby constellated:

                                                    weavers archers

goatherds

                        and the plough
                of names and shapes that burst

into us
(Choose from among
(My Lady, try on this one.

53

# May 19, 1435: The Great Freeze

It is reported he walked out

counted seven score birds
frozen to stone in the trees.
        (the severe
        (the *dure*

and counting in her sleep

the hundred and forty
the crystal trees.

Item: today (and for a quarter of that
year)

To sever of

seized

and the walking rock

you could see right through

# May 21, 1420: Signing the Treaty of Troyes

And thus we give up: This and this and

In a ceremony in which hands are severed, it's traditional to hire a choir, to
blind the neighbors, to refuse all letters

or you could simply pluck out my eyes, serve them up on a plate (some
saint already tried this) and I'll walk around reciting "Ok, I get it

Said Charles VI
and in signing found
that when he went to pick up the pen he couldn't remember whether he wrote
with his right hand or his left. It's permanent. They delivered a black granite cube
five meters high and stood it on his toe.
You get a great view from here; it just isn't yours anymore.

# May 30, 1427: Joan-not-yet-saint with Sheep

When they eat from your hand it's said that you're saved
or that you saved them.     You can never be sure.     What you heard.
                                                                                What did
And how          do you know it was Saints She and Her?
                                        And which them?
                                                              We ask you
to close your eyes and picture: night (held close, black & white). Men in
armor, the army at the gate.          And we haven't even begun to consider
what we really mean by mad.
And will make of it a king.                              We ask you to picture
men huddled around fire. There was so much less light then. And it glinted their
armored bodies into black bodies of water. The way things move
                              in uncertain light
is not to be discounted. A touch with
the tip of a finger on an otherwise sleeping forehead,
                                        between the eyebrows
                                        and up about half an inch. What
will you give.

# June 1: Reaping

Sickle one, scythe two and sweep and sheaf and sign
in the rocking field and the river whole
in its own         (what hold
           what
           boat

of the errance of a spire (despite appearance
               it's miles

(at the door of the river) (that curves into harvest

Choir: Let us
        harbor in this witness
                            a man
           with an oar
shreds a surface

(at the door he calls a river)

a person slipping inward

               How stone reigns
               How hay stings
               (How swing this scythe so I look a little less like
                                   my own death)
                               who
                           sings
                       of

Of all the towers on the castle, three are red.
What are they carrying in the boat?
(List everything you could carry
away in a boat.)

# June 2

The flight of red (the various

Flights
      though it's not
      what you had in mind
but a red
cap down an angled stair

there where three

there's the arm of a shirt

                  (we were so small a single word

It is commonly thought that many monastic orders of the 14th and 15th
centuries demanded silence. It is commonly thought

Rain falls.

It's June.
I'm dressed in red.
I'm falling.

I'm walking down a stair. It's not brick red, like the roofs, but brazened

open as if onto
the body room after room

Meet me
by the unused stair

that opens onto the river; you open the door and there, on the water
I was raised to a pious life

and cannot live here.

# Recipes for Red

ardor and pestle
igneous anchor
suckled on iron
and flaming just a little on parchment is the fevered
                  skin of animal: this

          was made to proof
          was boiled to world
          and powdered, pounded,
          chained. (Shaved with a shard of glass the great
blocks of brazilwood
                  *(colorus flammeus)* from the forests of Ceylon
and from there by sea to Alexandria in great quantity ('brazil' from 'brazier'
from
'bright waiting' stains the hands and they say the taste is slightly sweet.

While some of the most brilliant
were extracted from insects (the *coccus ilicis* as it dies upon the branch)

*kermes* from the Arabic made Latin *kermesinum* made Italian *cremesino,*
*cramoisie* in French and a brilliant crimson
          wakeful state
                  marginal conflagration
                          largely developed for the Florentine wool-trade.
He said:
How to make mercury from cinnabar through deprivation:
(the marriage of the former to sulphur
          and the heritage of vermillion:

          Oh *minium* ("to miniate") red sulphide of mercury
and *miltos* and *cinabrum, sandaracca*, orange tetroxide of lead called

a simple procedure: mix the mercury with the sulphur, stir twice, sneeze once
and heat the remainder.
Quicksilver and mortar.
Monsieur, will you do me the honor; take the blood from this faucet
and make from it a pair of gloves.

# June 15, 1416: The Death of Jean, Duc de Berry

Who had fallen in love in prison (1363) — the swan once wounded
hounds. How does it/how it does      go on
           nameless, veiled
parchment or veiled in parchment or never
has nor will      the sun upon this skin: porous,     my populous
      and aerial port
         (I had three sons
            all dead
            he said
            though that's much later
            and always too early)
        though the circumstances varied and from the
        second marriage, nothing.


The swans migrate past the cell window
       (the window narrow
       so the huge birds cross it
       one by one
           frame by frame        (almost growing)
or it's the same one passing     (enormous)       and in between
                            the sky.

# June 24: A Long Day

The day of Jean L'Amour. The "Saint-John"—all summer starts here. Lit
a fire on every corner. Rain of. Done. (and all the city alight with it. Ashes
bring honor,
aim peace, and anchor     *cendres*          *semance*     the senders
sooner or later
        a man shifts in his chair but keeps looking out the window


so rarely seen this time of year because
they have become in this time of war nocturnal things like the swans once
were when they could hover, could
tread air
                (representing the soul at peace etc. while in addition serving
as an early version of the streetlight—*Cygne—cendre—signer*—seer
of signs much later
became our word "singer." Now *sing*—Louder, I said, louder. I said
Soon.

# July 1: Field Geometry

all that interlocks is fawn                         all that water joins
                                    the sound
of a scythe and the sound of shears
                                    weather and mortar        the hand-made
air, that  geometry

like arithmetic, is now recognized as a liberal art
                    "indispensable to a country whose science has achieved"
field after field such fine tune
                    to the tones of shadow one blade
                    casts upon another
            diamond pasture
            mapped              trees      fan out
            fan-shaped, splayed grace, inverting the grasp, there in the
fractured
circle
traced by a sickle and its private arc from harvest to heart or a little
                        beyond, say, to the shoulder of the average man.

# July 2, 1421: A river of blood has flowed three days into the Seine

*In one this week*
in this now year
of all our after
a winter so long          and "so divers" below the bridge
                          at Saint Honoré was seen
a stream of blood flowing into the Seine as thousands watched began
                              (this means
                                   you could see into the river then)
they said
on the Sunday
                         how blood feathers out (the metaphors are rife)
(the does-not-stop
oh stopped in prayer. There's a plume
                    there's a flail        a sail turned upside down
threshing
three days on
a sign banging in the wind
                              will later become an entire army
and all their arms
Walking on water to victory, singing.

# July 3, 1418: The Miracle of Crime

When, coming home drunk, a Swiss soldier stabbed the stone statue of the Virgin
at the corner of the rue aux Ours and the rue Salle-au-Comte, blood poured out.
Even in the dark
to sudden such red

               So they flayed     (picture it)
him alive,
forced him to face
the carved image "from six
in the morning until his entrails left him."
                  And from then on marked the day
                  by a high mass and a stately procession
                  as seemed fit to honor
                  such *gloire de miracle*
                             that
Blood pours from stone (and in the torchlight, ore
                  but
                    that's another issue)     *So they flayed*
(Even in the dark,     such a lamp
leaps)    (such sudden    even

a dark lamp, a torch of burning gold, who'd never bled before
                                *him alive.*

# July 5, 1421: In Which the Plight

Of starving wolves
                (they dig up new graves (amid) (the winter's having been
                etc. (the summer turned) and all
and this
                (they call it) "maudit war"
is addressed.
(They choke on air.)
           One year they even took to entering
the city by swimming up the Seine
because of course the portes were barred and one
year one attacked
a "woman with child" eating first
the unborn and that
seemed to them worse than the death
of the mother who I say died twice because
and forced to watch there are wolves
in the river as the river is freezing over
they are swimming up the freezing river in droves.

# July 7

Because (it's said)                  seven heavenly bodies
                                  (the signs return) every seven hours
                                  seven days of the week—
                                  the seven wonders of the world that isn't

ancient and the
seven seals that keep them silent    and molten
                                  and if there
                                  were a future

who found seven faces
just coming into focus
                                  was all eyes
                                              (where)

were (and/or) are
                  seven veils


                  hide the signing
"Now" that would be a future (said,
pointing)        That
                is what
                      from effort might
            (the seven cataracts of not

and fall
asleep in the grass, white grass
invisible in the white light.

# July: Coquelicot

Folio sept: Verso. So it goes. There will be. All field. Entire they. The
purple flowers are never named.

Say: "We
the Precise, we
incise

and then slice.
It's timed
by the body, lean and
rise; rise and
the River Clain.
It is we
who believe, or is it I.
Tide. Sliding. Sky.
Though now we say *azura*, from which
the blue is made.

# August 1: The Outing

("All this shall someday be

                    Birds:
                                        Plane 1:
            Count them: 5
                                                    choreographed
a private alphabet:
one falconer
with his one red sock
                                (the fine
lady and her one red sleeve
sieve
                    one into a thousand days
                                        It's raining birds
who hunt birds, it's
always morning here.

## August 3: The tower in the background, named La Guinette, which is, by the way, still standing

Things had names.          Towers, jewels, swords. We vestige the gesture in
                           rivers: i.e., here the Juine. And watched over:
Means:
          Guin: look
          ette: out or "the Watcher"


was startled and turned too quickly. We were watching something
come up the road, still too far away to
                                        Who are these people who
ask the way      by name, who name
to whole this fragile hold.

# August 1424: The First Dance Macabre

Long line of arm in and          and there on the farthest wall we are
painted across the walls of          they were
soft burned within entwined          there's all this time
                    turning in the arms of
                              August          named the *danse Macabré*
after the painter          who lost          and were not


                    (innocent they say *we were* and
                                        (*Reach for us*
the "*cemitiere des*
                                        (You picture children fleeing a massacre where
          *innocents*" for
the shadow of the choir painted here          even there
                                                  where even
                                                  the condemned
(You dance and we'll sing.)
                              Last until Lent of the coming year.

## August 1427: Abundance

Item: this year:

               *and made so beautiful August that it made never of the age*

*of man alive*

*Comme* (as) *dit* (is) *est* (said):

               but in that little hour did God labor

                           and how it is *appert* = eyes

the color of wheat, the wheel

holding still as when anything thrown straight up stops,

hangs, free of its own weight for a split-second, split

can enter. Wealth of sudden fruit, call me

whatever you want.

# August 17, 1427: The first record of Gypsies in Europe

*sont arrivés*: twelve men from Basse Egypt

and then their hundred saying we
                                    were five thousand but seven
years sentenced to wander
were lodged outside the city for fear of

the word for ugly is the same as that for dark. Equals: arm in arm and the question
is, are they Christian? and what have they done with Egypt? and can we, too, wor-
ship the sun?

                                          pierced
                                          the ear
                    (sign of high birth)
                                          where the reclaimed were
                  (we all have one)
                                          or five or ten or
                                          who
      ever read   into your palm who    either said though I died it surely
                                          was
                                          is
                                          I
see you walking down a long road with enormous fields on either side, very
green.

# August 20, 1418: Famine with Rumors of War

from the root word "tend"

                       (tendence; tender; *tendu*)

          "to tendril" does this

deft twist on

            how much was left then     *disette*

of this little theft

of breath and a flagrant health hovered

starving

turns you blind.        All the with.

                  Caught.

                  Have


you turned to stone or sun? How many can you see through

disguised as shore.

73

# August 26, 1425

Item:
> They arm the blind. (Who were also the starved.)
Item: at least once, the blind were armed.
> > Were marched (four of them)
through the streets, but that was yesterday.
> > Now it's Sunday. They still have their clubs in hand
> > and a pig is placed (on a long chain) between them and
someone says
> > Whoever kills the pig will have all of him to eat. What an odd phrase, to say we "stand" something. All the neighbors stood by watching. The blind of course were beaten half to death. No one screamed, fled, or snapped suddenly mad. In fact, most were mildly entertained, and the rest just unusually tired.

# September 1.618: In Light of Gold

Light is the shadow of God. —Marsilio Ficino

## I. FIRE GILDING

The trick this time is mercury
rubbed in by hand, hand and chalice

                              being each other inverted
        It goes like this:
        bronze bonds first        to the quicksilver layer
        which then fuses to the leaves of gold
laid on by hand,        the electrons slip
        their orbit to enter
        and another planet
            swings into effort.

For centuries the sky was gold                we have the proof.

There were stars then, yes, of course, but who would have known
the        "heavenly body"
        had it been
        mercury burning
            had it        occasionally

            they often died inhaling

the gold beaten transparent
and laid on in whole sheets
roughly the shape of a door
        fell into place, into every
where is sun (they said) (was)
        then
        this huge        we
put it there.

75

## II. CHRYSOGRAPHY WITH GOLD INKS

        Refractory.
Ground the lens rubbing two fingers together: I am lonely,
my friend. Said
             on a background of endlessly variable greys
"St. Jerome
inveighed against the worldliness, extravagance,
the purple skins against which the gold words

and a man (he comes clothed in the body of the poor) naked
just outside the room

To burnish properly, lean in until the sweat
(the door is shut, a once-much-larger man

in the empty courtyard I am
coming through. I've heard you should
burnish with a tooth tied firmly to an oar.

## III. GILDING BY ATTRITION (for backgrounds)

you take ground glass (you grind glass)
               mix it with glair
      you paint with glass
      in itself
          some sky
some take
      a solid block
of gold and rub
the shards rip flakes

from your hand. Another
way to make sky
          is the stars that people the sky
          or the people or at least their eyes.

# September $3^2$

The ellipse that leads into
    (Sept.)
                (seven +
        the it & the not-it)
        the nine planets
        silent in their endless
(the seven known + the two nonexistent)
                (chunk of ice and the other simply gas and
what makes a

curve are lined the visions:
          ire, iron, ether
           ember, every, ivory
        eternity and isosceles, ides
abbreviated as:
        (iso)3 or
          $\Delta \rightarrow x \div \sqrt{3^2}$
if overall the form is taller than it is
we will come to live; if not
the surface of the water, shattered
into congruent panes
travels unconstrained by laws of nature. There is
no law to state this—
they turn over and over end over end
but the very fact of windows,
fixed or not, amid all that dark and the
nine grains of sand that began
the world, the nine windows of the face that fuse it into feral,
magnifying it as does
a shard of glass
dry grass in autumn.

# September 10, 1419:
# The Assassination of Jean sans Peur

In retaliation (see November 23)
kneeling in homage
it is shown occurring:
Choose a bridge in broad daylight, the Yonne drifting
by below while Tanguy du Châtel
simply kills him. Others lean
on the railing and watch. Everything looks
so peaceful in old illuminations; the sky
a pasture, and the action gently ushering us
toward the center of the picture, just as aesthetic theory
says it should, where a man stands
in a red hat, and behind him, a man dressed in red.

# September 21, 1431: Woman Loses Sleep

Early afternoon—many around—you know how those women
will stand about and gab  as Marie—notre héroïne—turning with her
                              bucket, heard
                              a fall
                              a long
whistled thing with others trailing behind
and then a cup-shaped sound, a some-thing water forever
                              and fearing it was her wedding ring slipping, she
                              touched
but there it was          and what else                    that small she lost
sleep for seven nights and then began a lifetime of dreaming
of falling. "A rest" she says "like one has never felt, and the extravagant
promise of an imminent earth."

# October 1, 1445

How to paint a filament designed to be invisible:
How to paint a white dog against a white wall:
How a world in stages, striated, calibrated:

first you notice a person walking, the river that rives     open the picture, the
three boats and the one man, the raised arm, the something in the hand.
Such a busy world ruled by birds, held down by stone,
                                        and holds. Sown:
Someone coming
through the arch of a doorway     into a world in which
shadow has so recently been invented *(1440–1450)* it stretches     My one
man reflected
for every man standing
on the edge of a river is a part of it.

# October 2

At the center of the picture, a river

cuts the picture in two. This is not the first time. You may have noticed

this straight line at the heart and the world doesn't meet

$\qquad\qquad\qquad\qquad\qquad\qquad$ *batel* = boat

$\qquad\qquad\qquad\qquad\qquad$ *atant:* to this point

$\qquad\qquad\qquad\qquad$ and *choir,* to fall down into

$\qquad\qquad\qquad$ each one, its wavering twin

the river offers

$\qquad\qquad\qquad\qquad$ of the river, sheer passage

$\qquad\qquad\qquad\qquad\qquad$ and ere in passing

$\qquad\qquad\qquad\qquad\qquad\qquad$ And during great rains

it retraces

$\qquad\qquad$ its primitive route, curving just below the hills of Belleville, and on
$\qquad\qquad$ toward Montmartre, making islands out of floods.

$\qquad\qquad\qquad\qquad\qquad\qquad$ "I'm a wishing mill"

$\qquad\qquad$ I'm a wedge between the ribs
$\qquad$ a peeled muscle exposed to sun

$\qquad\qquad\qquad\qquad\qquad$ cut in two. I would not choose.

# October: A Superstitious Hour

Nothing is     as is        seen
                                     still sees. And nothing seems
     only.     There lives

           Entire insides          a shifted mirror
                                  a much larger
                    a tithe
and in the tithe, an anchor. No simple man
plows without furrowing heaven
without feeling the earth beneath him
rest upon nothing:                   every bird, a word of God
                                   unless hawk = vengeance
                                   lark: that all is transient
           whereas a swallow in the morning means odd wealth, secret friends
a swallow in the evening, and you die a free man

For two days, a pheasant strutted around
the central market with no fear of being arrowed, skewered or stewed,
for it too knew that it alone kept hold of all the souls of
children dead in their first year, and when it failed to appear
on the third day, the women wept with joy and to a woman claimed
to have seen, whenever she glanced up, a face she no longer recognized.

# October 4, 1451: Nicholas of Cusa
# Preaches at Aix-la-Chapelle

*Mensurare temporalia fecit geometria spritualis.* —St. Antoine

Godar

        chi         tectan

dastro        nomer       et           enginer

alma         future

were clear

signs:

        heaven is an attribute of night

                  (as a segment of a circle's line
                    would be straight
                    were the circle infinite)

and now it's time to weigh the sun
    *"Mind is measure come to life"*
first weigh the plants that it has grown
divide by one
    *"achieves its potential in the measurement of"*

    (recorded seeing (February 1, 1425) a camel

    in a small town just over the German border

    a sliding planet
and its curving, path by path, forward nonetheless
                a cold seed
                    has a delicate shoulder seen
                    and would but could not
               be recorded or more
simply said that all things orbit, distracted, I
often find myself at home.

# October 7, 1434

Remembered for its gale—both of the two surviving accounts of this day
talk of nothing but
wind was, and thus, it seems
     solid weather
     (and not be wrong)  remains
           "Utter as fire, tore, I swear, whole
stones"
"heard voices"
     violently live, the mehanism that bends its limbs
back on themselves
     a quickened theft,   the weave
           left, woven
           flown into new
flying things, took
a crossbeam at least four *toises* long some fifty feet
and laid it down on a garden gate, balancing. I swear I saw this
with my eyes.

# October 12, 1492: The Death of Piero della Francesca and the Error in Perspective

                         a child
the size of the
palm of the
                    hand the size of

                    slightly
bent rays
                    —sill, tile, altar, all
architecture ends in the face of Christ
                              is a city
                              says
                              you cannot make it come to life
unless it's properly off
even into twisted unto huge
in the corner of the apse   a monstrous grace

from on Earth
looks safe.

# Fortune, The *Boccaccio* of Jean sans Peur, 1409–1419

We know our monsters only—not *par l'entremise des anciens textes*—but by the
direct witness of travelers. Have seen. And they did
                          tend to surpass
                 nothing at all like it              most of us
                       dream of people and horror
is human in form. Most of us
                 credulous, vary it a bit         Marco Polo, for instance, was
the first to see living beings with so many faces and "some have four, others
twenty, and others up to one hundred hands. (The more hands (it was thought)
the more likely you were to be telling the truth.)
and others up to
                   We're waiting.            We're standing
on streetcorners counting
while Fortune (looking remarkably like the Virgin) sits chatting
to a Donor, is adorned (à la Shiva) with an arm for every one.
It's said they moved,     so many mills
                   in the wind are yet other
futures, but they refuse.

# October 15, 1415: Guild Initiation: Paolo Uccello Examines the Sky

Vasari swears

         the birds were there, are

    still

      beware      they are

           the hand

rose to the face to brush
away what was there that was

         difficult, was

still half-unmade

a truce implied by flight

    A man walks out of a painting into a war
and all that should be there
is there

      and what should not

ever, it's      now all over
it's the animals that fly
it's that now
the hunted      sail for a minute

# The Machine Designs

still thin, though straight, the     between
                    The.     We
tend to forget kinship         ticks            connects
clocks to astronomy. It's not really so surprising and enormous and (you
search for the word) nested, or scaled or something I suppose
any life is pierced.
all these things that pass right through     light    axes    zone
upon zone: Mark you well                 and there you'll be,
                        marked. The oldest
clock is the dark. The closest, a heart.
Why work?
We're here for good.
One plate slips
behind the other
and you hear the shift
as a short 'i'—i.e., *sill, lip, shipping*.

# October 25, 1415: The Battle of Agincourt

Having promised to cut three fingers
off the right hand of every archer
                    on the map
                    between the small
                    soft trees,
                    ten thousand men.

# October 28, 1449: The Translation of the Relics of St. Jean in Anticipation of the End of the Hundred Years' War

Is over

          that has ever been told

don't count.

          *Les revenants* do here
          so sovereignly hold
          my hand who sees in the dark

          is now heard
          the work of peace of
shoal, bank, rive, shore, grève

They were fifty thousand strong in the rue Saint-Martin
who said
The story of a hundred years long
who said
they come back at all?
will be loved.

# November 1: All Saints' Day

St. (Breathe)
      known by his (guess) St. (Yes) known by
(in my wildest, please) (and I would have) St. Always
recognized by his hands (the man had fifteen hands) St.
How ever did you St. Yet live on          Still depicted with
     1) her flaming dragon
     2) her flying candle
     3) her drowning candle
     4) her dragon in tears
     5) St. Who-with-her-heart-in-her-hand (that would be Catherine of
Sienna (Giovanni di Paolo, c. 1420) holds out
her heart clutched is of course red but what may seem odd is the comic shape that
will someday anoint all those bumperstickers or is it adorn? already perfectly
formed
exchanges her heart with Christ
who does what in return? How odd to have forgotten that

And St. Jerome with his lion, his book, and his rock,
and St. Jerome in his desert, which is always his own, and
St. Jerome poised forever on the threshold of the beautiful world.
In Antonella's *St. Jerome*, he is seated in a room whose architecture emulates
the chambers of the heart.

# November 2: All Souls' Day

Walk again         have passed this gate        at night and
landscape
     (that white thing)
          done:
          does,
          lives,
          *is*
          the unreeling body
And so on       is the *on*.      Walking is a holy thing; it sieves the sun.

# November 3

Jean Colombe. Stole from the cathedrals of Auxerre,
Bourges, Chartres, Poitiers, and Sens
cette homme.
Vitraux (such a lovely word) and in the window
stands
a man who once held Saint Luke in his arms.
This oh my prodigal son
to have turned to what

a hand once white
a white now seeps
up from the bone
a repetitious hum
Have we as well
the magnetic pearl
that pulls the birds
from sky to sky I amble
from room to room I hear
that you were and whittle
some bitter

Liked November, the number 11, the water at a given distance, and no castle
but that hidden by trees.

# November 9, 1414: Margery Kempe Marries God

Who is they     we
       say (they said)
tear

                 and the turning form,
                 blindfolded, being
                 so quickly turned around) I have been
crying now for seven thousand years
                 against *the sownd of the Holy Gost like a peyr of belwys blowyng*
changed
(and I leave this book)
           now      *the voys, the dowe, the song ful merily in the ryth ere*
now and wander: if God had an acre and three sons all born of different
women in the same minute of the same day of the same year
who
shall inherent you and forfeit the earth.
Fourteen children, and only one whose name I now remember because he was
a sinner and whenever he came home laughing
                            "I am
                            the pilgrim

          of the sign of the leaving
all the way to Jerusalem                 kicking and screaming
                               in the holy seeing
in the ghostly comfort of a teetering heaven
                               attended
by the wedded: *"Dowtyr, I wil han ye*     "waiting for the touch, the hand
                               raised
to the other hand held up            and one wonders as one waits

          about incidental things, about the time it takes, and then about space,
          the way it curves to fit the most intricate of them.

# November 11, 1422: The Funeral of Charles the Sixth, the Mad, and the Beloved

*le visage découvert*
and the naked face
retraced a route it had never traveled unaided before. The people sobbed
                    thousands of belief
          beneath a canopy of gold
the face stared at the peeled sun.
Followed by a banquet to which literally all Paris was invited and were told to take
all they wanted, to eat and drink with their eyes, their hands, their entire arms in an
excess of grief because peace can only be won by the mad have lost the war have
drunk the well and for once in our lives could ask for more.

## November 1485: Jean Colombe Hands the
## Finished Manuscript to Charles I of Savoy

And from there four hundred years
                                hidden in air
                                seemed huge
when slipped through a hole and there are worlds
that float.
                        Count the lives:
                        7, 6, 5
                        4, 3, 2
                                They say the universe is curved
like the palm of a hand
like a jawline reflected in water
like sand.

After the death of the Duc de Berry, the unfinished manuscript went to his sole
heir, King Charles VI, and from there to Duc Charles I of Savoy. It then disap-
peared until 1855 when Henri d'Orléans, Duc d'Aumale heard of it and traced it to
a girls' boarding school in Genoa. Coats of arms on the binding indicate that it was
owned at some point by the Spinola family and then later by the Marquis Hieron-
ymous Serra of Genoa.

There are holes in the          (What is this
                    sky
                                all over my hands?)

                        At the back of the eye, an infinitesimal window
that doesn't close.

The sound of thread. He woke up. He wakes up.
We remember it because it was an uncommonly beautiful day; one that makes you
say, "This—

was later found somewhere else.

## November 23, 1407: The Murder of
## Louis d'Orléans in the rue Vieille-du-Temple

Murdered: one brother
of a mad king of
        a lover of
        the queen             traceried in power
and in plans for obtaining power. We watch the laurel
colored fields and equal hills get endless *Oise, Marne*, herds, such
who wouldn't for this         risk
            what âme
one might find behind a door
            no other land so
on your knees you
surrounded him and beat him to death.

# November 25: St. Catherine's Day

Wheels! (see page *yeah, sure* first invented in and
       St. Catherine how pale you are and broken at your feet (cf. spinning
lathe
turning crank
mill wheel
and water mill
and married Christ in his mother's arms (cf. wheel of vanes
       a veritable fan-escapement
slowing time or at least the sound
when the hour strikes and scrapes the air.

(see here)                    (cf. a scar
crossing an eye) (see, they say there's a clock in every cell

see: wheel of bells, cranked, one
of the earliest uses, perfect meld of recognitions, to wit, wheels and clocks,
and how they came
to have faces. What they mean when they say
don't turn around—
Let me tell you what they did with wheels.

Faces
scraped against sky

in which

and spins; and there were
simple mills
and the mules walked in circles

coming around

after the anaesthesia/trance
a simple speaking in tongues

then thought that it would make
a map, a perfect
had in mind a hand, fisted, that if
perfected, if could turn, what a shape
for the coming world: a leaf on a pond in the wind.
Water
water
my homuncular bead.

# November 25

There is perfect weather; you can smell it,
and no color will ever be this color, these colors—
It's Thanksgiving, and a perfect Thanksgiving Day with a
soft focus on the laws of nature and thousands
of people on their knees on the sidewalks, eyes closed,
heads thrown back and talking quietly to each other.

# December 0: New Math

How feared it was        this certain
        gap in the ceiling        a wholly beckoning
at the heart of the new
                Hindu-Arabic system: the zero means not
needing
and counting
the not
so quickly that
        one enormous now
without end
once there was


        and the egg was empty
        acre in and into
        entire rooms, whole towns, our mouths.

# December 1: The Hunt

to every month
its animal
animal

rhythm the regular                 to rhigulum

To build a metronome
                                   (rest a counterpulse)
                                   (set)
        offset, for instance
        pending, suspended in its always
as long as

Count them.
But it's the heart that does that. That's its job; it counts
every instant of an animal's life and almost makes it equal

# December 12

And when God thought
        said St. A. he thought
8 + 4 means time is here
                        arrived
                                achieved: (the Alexandrine proof) there
were twelve
tribes in Israel, twelve apostles to follow twelve signs
that lurk between sky and heaven
                        and if you add up
the spatial world (four cardinal points, four seasons, and four elements and
if each planet had a ghost
                                and if two got lost
or so the saint explained: the finger missing from each hand and don't you
find
                you're always slightly
thinking of it.

# December 24

Before birth
          *ex Patre* (was the) *Patris* (lumière the père:
                  *Tu lumen*
      (you have left the
who was your
intime
for *saecula saeculorum*

as it was in the beginning
and on him flowered : my soul attending:
          *anima mea in verbo ejus*
                       watches the horizon
      (abundance
will redeem it
        (pay attention
   did ransom

      *ANTIPHONE:*
      *Know that the kingdom of God*
      *is as we say at Hand    and attached*
      *at the wrist,    this world    bends in the light*
curves
      *hunc caelum veritas* siècle de futur
      *pacificus*
and the alliance de miraculous et *omnibus*, this paix and this coeur
      whose blood washed the stars    (that's a question
            (a riddle, an anagram
     for eyelid
        mansion
        and/or
            washed in the blood of a turnip,
this infant
born perfect with perfectly formed hands of glass
     *Gloria Filio!*
     across les siècles
     that licked them clean.

# December 25, 1456: Je Françoys Villon, escollier

It's snowing

           bitter

       ground

to dust

and salt

       will shudder in the heel:

              a broken window


"It's I who steals from churches

                       who reaps the learnèd sequence

                             who says

          (I was made for loving

my only

Joan of Act)

here in my hand

                *(I bequeath the beautiful theft*

                *La Lanterne de la rue Pierre-au-Lait*

all my names

        tooth after tooth

                phalanxed to snow         no

                      night

             boned

       black

(they say) (no, it was I)

who said when wolves live on wind they get fat.

# December 28: Day of the Saints-Innocents

Were not counted

We lost count

     You can't get children that young to march
     you can't even get them to run

He said every male child under

and all the others who by error or abyss     (dismantled dust by dust)
     get lumped into this     day of infant saints (and the day after next
        in come the actors, scene by scene and room by room;
we happen again: *officium*
*pastorum. officium stelle. ordo Rachelis.*     and every time
the plague returned, will see this theme take deeper root yet more delicate,
intricate, the features more precise,
more like someone
you knew or might have known     but for the war
     this day alone
     the dead exceed their number
and was wrongly slain.

the dead who cede their number

the dead released from number and wrongly

the dead in their number beyond number

the dead alone understand number and
the dead alone number
the dead, utter in their number, and wrong.

# List of Sources

*Journal d'un Bourgeois de Paris de 1405 à 1449*. Paris: "Lettres Gothiques," Le Livre de Poche, 1990.

Baltrusaitis, Jurgis. *Le Moyen Age Fantastique*. Paris: Flammarion, 1981.

Cazelles, R. *Les Très Riches Heures du Duc de Berry*. Paris: Seghers, 1988.

Cennino d'Andrea Cennini. *The Craftsman's Handbook*, trans. Daniel Thompson, Jr. New York: Dover, 1960.

Collis, Louis. *Memoirs of a Medieval Woman: The Life and Times of Margery Kempe*. New York: Harper, 1983.

Crosby, Alfred W. *The Measure of Reality*. Cambridge University Press, 1997.

Delort, Robert. *La Vie au Moyen Age,* third edition. Paris: Éditions du Seuil, collection "Points Histoire," 1982.

Duby, Georges, editor. *A History of Private Life Vol. II*, trans. Arthur Goldhammer. Cambridge, Mass.: Harvard, 1988.

Eco, Umberto. *Art and Beauty in the Middle Ages*, trans. Hugh Bredin. New Haven: Yale University Press, 1986.

Edgerton, Samuel Y., Jr. *The Heritage of Giotto's Geometry*. Ithaca: Cornell University Press, 1991.

Farmer, David. *The Oxford Dictionary of Saints*, fourth edition. Oxford: Oxford University Press, 1997.

Field, J. V. *The Invention of Infinity*. Oxford University Press, 1997.

Geremek, Bronislaw. *The Margins of Society in Late Medieval Paris*, trans. Jean Birrell. Cambridge University Press, 1987.

Grant, Edward. *The Foundations of Modern Science in the Middle Ages*. Cambridge University Press, 1996.

Heers, Jacques. *Fêtes des fous et carnavals*. Paris: Hachette/Pluriel, 1995.

Henish, Bridget Ann. *The Medieval Calendar Year*. University Park: Pennsylvania State University, 1999.

Hollier, Denis, editor. *A New History of French Literature*. Harvard, 1989.

Huizinga, Johan. *The Autumn of the Middle Ages*, trans. Rodney J. Payton and Ulrich Mammitzsch. University of Chicago Press, 1996.

Landsberg, Sylvia. *The Medieval Garden*. London: British Museum Press.

Schacherl, Lillian. *Très Riches Heures: Behind the Gothic Masterpiece*, trans. Fiona Elliott. Munich and London: Prestek-Verlag, 1997.

Seward, Desmond. *The Hundred Years War*. New York: Atheneum, 1978.

Siraisi, Nancy G. *Medieval and Early Renaissance Medicine*. University of Chicago Press, 1990.

Thompson, Daniel V. *The Materials and Techniques of Medieval Painting*. New York: Dover, 1956.

Vasari, Giorgio. *The Lives of the Artists*, trans. Julia Conaway and Peter Bondanella. Oxford University Press, 1991.

Verdon, Jean. *La Nuit au Moyen Age*. Paris: Hachette/Pluriel, 1997.

White, Lynn, Jr. *Medieval Technology and Social Change*. London: Oxford University Press, 1962.

Wieck, Roger S. *Painted Prayers*. New York: George Braziller, Inc., and the Pierpont Morgan Library, 1997.